James Ramsay

Objections to the Abolition of the Slave Trade

With Answers to which are Prefixed Strictures

James Ramsay

Objections to the Abolition of the Slave Trade
With Answers to which are Prefixed Strictures

ISBN/EAN: 9783744742092

Printed in Europe, USA, Canada, Australia, Japan

Cover: Foto ©ninafisch / pixelio.de

More available books at **www.hansebooks.com**

OBJECTIONS

TO THE

Abolition of the Slave Trade,

WITH

ANSWERS.

OBJECTIONS

TO THE

Abolition of the Slave Trade,

WITH

ANSWERS.

TO WHICH ARE PREFIXED,

Strictures on a late Publication, intitled,
" Confiderations on the Emancipation of
" Negroes, and the Abolition of the Slave
" Trade, by a Weft India Planter."

By the Rev. JAMES RAMSAY, A. M.

———————

LONDON:

Printed and Sold by James Phillips, George-Yard,
Lombard-Street.
M.DCC.LXXXVIII.

INTRODUCTION,

THE following Objections to the Abolition of the Slave Trade, with Anſwers, were intended to give a ſummary view of that ſubject. Theſe objections being collected from various perſons and writings, there will be found in them no ſmall degree of contradiction, for which the collector is not anſwerable. But whatever they may be, they have all been advanced by different people, with a view to produce an effect on perſons who have not ſtudied the ſubject; and they are therefore neceſſarily brought together here, to be ſeparately examined and weighed. If every anſwer be not found equally concluſive, the candid reader will remember that it is a ſingle perſon, who endeavours to give him a view of a very extenſive ſubject, which takes in a variety of conſiderations.

Since this plan was reſolved on, a publication has appeared in favour of the ſlave trade, which, coming at once fairly to the queſtion, claims a particular attention. It is intitled, Conſiderations on the Emancipation of the Negroes, and on the Abolition of the Slave Trade, by a Weſt Indian Planter; and is affirmed by the Monthly Reviewers to be invincible, on political grounds.

I ſhall firſt obſerve, that where this author treats of a general or partial emancipation of ſlaves, he combats a ſhadow; becauſe the preſent plan aims

A   only

only at the abolition of the African flave trade. It meddles not with flaves already in the colonies; if it did, that fympathy, which firft incited me to plead their claim to better treatment, would force me to range myfelf on the author's fide, and proteft againft the indifcreet meafure. All our flaves are not yet generally in a ftate, wherein full liberty would be a bleffing. Like children, they muft be reftrained by authority, and led on to their own good. But it would be infidious not to declare, that humanity looks forward to full emancipation, whenever they fhall be found capable of making a proper ufe of it. But this may be left to the mafter's difcretion. He who can procure a freeman to work for him, will never employ a flave: for the firft does twice the work of the other; and when he dies, his place is fupplied in the natural courfe of generation, not at an enormous expenfe from the flave-market. See my Effay, p. 118, &c. In Pennfylvania, where flaves are farther advanced in civilization, the Quakers have tried this experiment with the moft complete-fuccefs. Among many others, one man has freed 100 flaves, and finds his work better done, and his profits greater, for having divefted himfelf of this unnatural property. Indeed, what doth a peafant reap from his labour, which a flave ought not to receive, food, raiment, and neceffaries, to enable him to raife up labourers for his employers. But there is a confidence, a charm in liberty, that doubles his exertion, and foftens its toil. While increafing his employer's wealth, he provides for his family, and when his tafk is finifhed, his time is his own; no capricious tyrant intermeddles with his joy. Farther, the Britifh legiflature fhould be cautious how it meddles with the ftate of flaves in the colonies, left, while attempting

tempting to regulate their treatment, it confirm the bonds of flavery. If regulations be neceſſary, the iſland aſſemblies ſhould enforce them. While Britain gives them a monopoly of her ſugar market, ſhe will always preſerve a check over them. But if emancipation be not intended, the claim to the compenſation of £60,000,000 connected page 5. with it, is cut off. We have only to conſider' how far the abolition of the flave trade will affect the planter's property, in ſuch a manner as ſhall intitle him to compenſation. But the argument reſts on a foundation, that I truſt will not be allowed: he ſays, page 3, " That the planter poſ-
" ſeſſes a political right to his flave, whatever
" may be his moral right, and muſt be paid ac-
" cording to the flave's value, before his right can
" be extinguiſhed by reſtoring the flave to his
" natural freedom." This plea is not good. A horſe has been fairly bought in an open market, eſtabliſhed by authority: but he had been ſtolen, and the right owner diſcovers and claims him, and the thief is gone off. Muſt the right owner repay the fair purchaſer his price; or will this laſt be allowed to keep him? Still a horſe is an object of property; but when the queſtion is fairly agitated, I deny that a man can ever be an object of property, except in the caſe of an atrocious crime, which applies not to one flave in a thouſand, and excludes all children: the act that reduces him to flavery, is illegal and unjuſt; for it is impoſſible for a flave to receive a compenſation for his liberty.

A band of robbers may agree in ſtealing horſes, for each man to keep thoſe ſeized by him. This is binding on them, but not on the right owner, whenever he can aſſert his claim. In like manner, one flave-holder may preſcribe againſt another

A 2   flave

flave-holder, for the ufe of a flave; but he can make out no right when humanity lays in her claim; nor can he demand compenfation. Still, whatever be the claims of humanity here they are not enforced. In whatever manner the planter has acquired his flaves, no one intends to difturb him in the quiet poffeffion. We only aim to prevent his dealing in them, as far as it encourages robbers and murderers to carry on an inhuman traffick in the bodies of our fellow-creatures, which, as we fhall plainly fhew, will ultimately only ruin himfelf, if he perfeveres in it. And can he come in fuch a cafe to government for relief, and fay, Hitherto I have been allowed to buy from man-ftealers, wretched flaves to toil without recompence, without food, without cloathing, for my profit; if you take this privilege from me, on which I have depended, on which I have hazarded my fortune, you muft make good all my loffes as I fhall ftate them, even to the amount of £60,000,000?

The cafe is fairly ftated, murder and robbery are not on this fubject exaggerated terms. The nature thereof cannot be explained without them. And can " a political right" be oppofed to this reafoning? Can the planter's property be preferved to him, only by means that the feeling heart fhrinks from the difcuffion of? Perifh for me fuch confiderations! As a moral agent, as a member of a Chriftian community, I am not afhamed to maintain, and I truft I am not fingular in my opinion, that no political right ought to be fuftained, which is not founded on morality and juftice.

The flave has a natural right to freedom. Could we replace him where flavery found him, he ought to be returned to that fituation. But we cannot reftore his cottage, his family, his relations,

his

his country. If born a flave, we cannot often make him worthy of being a freeman. The only recompence we can make, is to treat him with confideration, and receive in return fuch fervice from him, as leaves him the reafonable enjoyment of himfelf. But becaufe we have already deprived his country of millions, which have been facrificed to our avarice, are we, for any argument that avarice or politics can adduce, to go on to murder and to deftroy? Is moral reafoning, is equal juftice, of fo little confequence among us, as on this ungenerous ground to be fet wholly afide? My candid adverfary will blufh, when he views this truly horrid bufinefs in this light; and even if the traffick were as valuable as he eftimates it, would fpurn from him wealth, that muft be acquired and kept by fuch methods. To do as we wifh to be done by, is the dictate of natural juftice, as well as of Chriftianity. We cannot lay in a claim to the attributes of humanity, if we deny its influence.

But, p. 11. This point of political right is given up; for he fays, " if the abolition were general, " nothing could be more falutary, becaufe every " nation would be left in its relative fituation." But if it be a right general meafure, it is a right meafure in refpect of us. We are not accountable for, we are not concerned in, the conduct of others; if there be any connection, it may be fafely left to the management of adminiftration. Our planters cannot be interefted in it, while they enjoy the monopoly of the Britifh market, where the price is higher than in any other place, and the demand increafes fafter than they can increafe their produce. And fo much perfuaded am I (as I fhall make appear) of their being able to keep up, or even increafe the prefent produce of fugar from

A 3   the

the number of flaves now in the colonies, without any new importation, that did they prove unable to fupply the market, I fhould be induced to charge it to their mifmanagement, rather than allow a compenfation; and fhould propofe ports to be opened in the Weft-Indies, for the introduction of as much foreign fugar, as would make good the deficiency. Thus fugar would be kept at a moderate price to the confumer; our fhipping would continue to be employed, and our revenue need fuffer no injury. We do this in a fcarcity of grain, why not alfo in a fcarcity of fugar. But this remedy will only be neceffary, fhould the planter wear his flaves out (as the author, p. 7, fuppofes) by ill treatment and feverity.

Farther, p. 33. he fays, " If planters were al-
" lowed time to prepare for the event, by ftock-
" ing their eftates to the full extent of their de-
" mands, the flave trade might be abolifhed."
Now while the flave market is open, inconfiderate planters, from their eagernefs to pufh on the culture of their eftates farther than it will profitably go, will continue to have demands on it. I folemnly affirm, that as often as I have heard the queftion concerning the buying or breeding of flaves difcuffed among planters, the preference has always been given to buying. The reader will determine what encouragement to population may be expected where this opinion prevails. And the fact in my time was, that nothing raifed a manager's refentment fooner, than to be informed that a negrefs was with child. I include not every manager; many are worthy humane men; I give it only as the prevailing opinion in this cafe. But a pofitive abolition of the flave trade will bring the planter to a fenfe of his intereft. Ufelefs domeftics will be turned into the field.
One

One third of the number of hired fervants will fully fupply their place. The fmall number of thefe laft, will allow them to be well fed on a part of the prefent expenfe of domeftic flaves, and their wages will be a fmall proportion of the fum which goes annually to purchafe new flaves.

But, p. 16. It is allowed, that " where the " planter is unencumbered, or has fufficient " ftrength, there the ftock may be kept up from " the births." The number in this fituation muft be confiderable. Every Weft-Indian family re-fiding in Britain muft be reckoned in it. For only the overplus revenue, after providing for the plantation, can be fpent here. Therefore a great part of the £60,000,000, claimed for ruined planters, will be faved in this clafs. Of involved planters, I affirm, that not one will be recovered from ruin by any purchafe of new flaves at their prefent advanced price. When Long, near twenty years ago, wrote his Hiftory of Jamaica, vol. 2. p. 437. fuch purchafes only involved him farther in debt. Slaves are now almoft one third dearer; the expenfe of fupporting them is increafed. Without taking into account the frequent accidents of hurricanes and bad crops, new flaves do not repay their firft coft, intereft, expenfe, and re-duction of number in feafoning.

Again, p. 26. It is faid, that " generally fpeak-" ing, every Weft Indian planter will affirm fla-" very to be an evil; it is juft to prevent negroes " from being enflaved." Then let us do what is juft, and leave the iffue to a watchful Providence. If flavery be an evil, if it be unjuft to enflave ne-groes, he is in a dangerous fituation, who by his demand of them encourages this injuftice, and promotes this evil. That politician, who, p. 27, is faid to be " unable to fquare his conduct by

A 4   " moral

(8)

" moral rectitude," will affuredly come fhort of his purpofe. Suppofe in this enlightened age, it were propofed to fit out a fquadron to go up the Baltic, to land parties to murder thofe who refift, to feize on the helplefs, to bribe the natives to kidnap each other, to be brought over tied neck and heels to work in our coal mines ; there is not a pretence for the prefent flave trade, for carrying on the manufacture of fugar, that may not be ufed here. It employs fhipping, it faves our own people from a deftructive employment; and if the Germans be warlike and oppofe us, it will exercife us in arms. But if we fpurn at this new fcheme, becaufe iniquitous and violent, why is the flave trade efteemed lefs violent and iniquitous, for having been the practice of two centuries ? Do we ufe the woman's argument for fkinning eels alive, that the Africans are accuftomed to it ? Whatever may be the cafe of their country or race, individuals are not accuftomed to it. To each unhappy wretch, it is a new, a fatal ftroke, that carries him away for ever from his native fpot, and determines and fixes his mifery. Habit cannot contribute to make it tolerable. They fink under the anguifh, and are loft for ever to fociety and themfelves.

Nor can the good confequences of this horrid trade be pleaded in extenuation of its cruelties. From comparing the numbers imported into the colonies, with the number of Creoles left, it is plain not one African in ten leaves pofterity behind him. But the value of a Creole flave, which is the only lafting good from importation, will be dearly purchafed at the expenfe of ten new flaves. And if a new flave will neither repay his expenfe by his labour, nor leave a profitable pofterity behind him, why is he purchafed ? Why adds the

planter

planter this unproductive bargain to his former incumbrances? Why is he concerned in a cruel traffick that cannot profit him; that muſt undo him?

I am ſorry to obſerve, p. 13. the following ſentiment in this candid writer: " Negroes are bought not for population, but for work; which, if not done, muſt ruin their owners." The concluſion is, that as the owner will not willingly ruin himſelf, the negroes muſt be worked at all hazards, and as " their condition expoſes them to accidents conducing to depopulation, their numbers muſt decreaſe." The meaning is, ſugar muſt be made, at the expenſe of the ſlave's life. Suppoſing this for a moment of thoſe already ſlaves, is Britain to be charged with the expenſe of £60,000,000, becauſe it forbids its own citizens any longer to commit robbery and murder, to ſupply ſlaves, who are profeſſedly to be worked down unprofitably in the making of ſugar. But why muſt the culture of the cane be conducted in a way, that admits not of an attention to the feelings of thoſe employed in it? Are the claims of nature, and the cravings of civilization ſo irreconcileable as to deſtroy one another? It is acknowledged, p. 7. that " ſlaves, where not worked beyond their ſtrength, are hearty, happy, and breed faſter." P. 11. 24. that " the abolition of the ſlave trade, if general, would leſſen the evils of ſlavery, and make the breeding and preſervation of ſlaves more an object of attention." If theſe be the genuine effects of ſuch a plan, what claim can he have on government, who, from a ſhort-ſighted love of gain, puſhes his ſlaves beyond their ſtrength, and deſtroys his property and proſpects together? Let him

him meet with execration from every feeling heart, and fall unpitied !

But from various examples in the different islands, it is evident that exceffive exertions have not in one cafe in an hundred produced immediate profit; and that to keep the work of flaves within their ftrength is the beft rate of employing them, the moft profitable way of cultivating a plantation. The number of fick, dead, and runaways, the liftleffnefs of thofe who remain, foon reduce the greateft exertions far below what might be got out of the gang with cheerfulnefs and eafe. In every inftance, and they have been numerous within my obfervation, this pufhing method defeated its own immediate purpofe. The quantity of work performed overpowers not the flave; but the time he is kept drawling at it, which leaves him no indulgence, no leifure to reft his wearied limbs. He might do much more in half the time. Therefore, if planters, on the abolition of the flave trade, refolve, as is fuppofed, p. 15. " to perfevere in making forced exertions," they will have themfelves to thank for the confequent ruin. Parliament can difpofe better of the public money, than in making good their lofs.

I fhall now confider the immediate effects of the abolition of the flave trade on the planter's property, the revenue, &c. We will fuppofe, with the confiderations, p. 4. that the plantation flaves are worth 20 millions, and the planters other property is equal to 40 millions, in all 60 millions. We will eftimate the whole annual plantation produce of fugar, cotton, coffee, &c. to be equal to 250,000 hhds. of Mufcovado fugar, worth in the colonies 17l per hhd. (their fuperiour value in Britain feldom exceeding freight, infurance, and other expenfes) or £. 4,250,000.

Suppofe

Suppofe the current annual expenfes of plantation ftores, managers, overfeers, agents, furgeons falaries, taxes, feeding, cloathing of flaves, to be £5 per head on half a million of flaves and white people employed on or about plantations, or £2,500,000. We trade with Africa for 40,000 flaves annually. The Confiderations, p. 30. fuppofe one half fold to our planters. Twelve years ago prime flaves fold for £48. They are not become cheaper. But fuppofe them when fold by the lot £43, the annual fupply of 20,000 will coft £860,000. Long, vol. 2. p. 482. fays, they are not ufeful till after three years. Three years intereft muft then be added. The intereft in the colonies varies from 10 to 6 per cent. Little money is lent to planters without a premium; or what is worfe, confignments of fugar. Suppofe the intereft 7 per cent.; three years intereft is £180,600. At the three years end, the 20,000 flaves will have coft £1,040,000. This, added to annual expences, leaves £710,000 for the returns of a capital of 60 millions; fomething better than one per cent. This is the profit of the manufacture which we are folicited to fupport.

The flaves in all our colonies, taking thofe in Jamaica from a late eftimate, and fuppofing the other iflands to have lately decreafed 40,000, may be reckoned 450,000. Of thefe the Creoles muft make 350,000; and among them the proportion between the fexes follows the courfe of nature. The African flaves, of which the greater part is male, cannot exceed 100,000. For thefe all die in fifteen years, and one third in the firft three years. But, about twelve years ago, the war put almoft an entire ftop to their importation; fo that four-fifths of all purchafed before that time

muft

muſt be dead ; and ſince the return of peace, the trade has been chiefly turned to the ſupply of St. Domingo. It is remarkable, that in this iſland, in the ſix years preceding 1774, there had been introduced 103,000 African ſlaves, and 61,728 had been born, making together 164,728; of which in 1774, there remained in all 40,000. To return, ſuppoſe theſe 450,000 ſlaves rented. Their rent and inſurance would, at the low rate of £10 per head be £4,500,000, which exceeds their whole produce, and leaves nothing for the returns of lands, &c. worth 40 millions more. Such is the property which parliament is called on to make good. We will take it in the moſt favourable point of view. If the planter pays his annual current expenſes, and ſupports his ſtock, all except negroes, out of a ſum equal to the rum, coffee, &c. and ſuch a part of the ſugar as leaves for the return of his capital £12 per hhd. on the ſugar alone, he is tolerably well ſatisfied. An ordinary crop of ſugar is about 160,000 hhds. at £12 or £1,920,000. Strike off £920,000 for the ſupply of ſlaves, we have one million for the returns of a capital of 60 millions, or about 1¼ per cent. If any plantation requires no ſupplies, then the returns are about 3 per cent. But not one half of the plantations ſupport themſelves, or make any returns on their capitals, this will allow a certain proportion to make 4, 5, or ſome few 8 per cent. on their capital ; but only if they buy no new ſlaves.

Long tells us, vol. 2. p. 437. 438. that the proportion of two hhds. of ſugar to three ſlaves, all ages included, is the utmoſt quantity they ſhould be made to produce, if the planter wiſhes to keep up or increaſe them from the births. It is indeed a greater proportion than the colonies at
preſent

prefent fupply; and therefore the flaves ought to increafe from the births. Suppofe thefe three flaves valued only at £ 50 each; (though, twelve years ago, I have known gangs, including all ages, valued at £ 60) or £ 150. The lands or property occupied by them are worth double, or £ 300. The two hhds. of fugar produced by the three flaves, after providing above for every expenfe, except new flaves, are worth £ 24. But the intereft of the three flaves, and other property occupied by them at 6 per cent. is £ 27. The infurance of the flaves at 5 per cent. is £ 7 10s. in all, £ 32 10s. the lofs is £ 8 10s. Suppofe the flaves rented: rent and infurance is now feldom fo low as £ 12 per head; take it only at £ 10, or on three flaves £ 30. Here is a lofs on them of £ 6, and no return on the lands, &c. worth £ 300; which, at 6 per cent. are worth £ 18. In thefe calculations, no allowance is made for hurricanes or bad crops, or high intereft; and in feveral colonies, the proportion of fugar is fet too high. Barbadoes contains 64,000 flaves. After allowing for the current expenfes, its produce is not £ 4 for each flave, without fuppofing any returns for lands, &c. worth 6 millions. Montferrat contains 9000 flaves, and makes 3000 hhds. of fugar, or one hhd. for three flaves. Here alfo can be no returns for lands, &c. worth one million. Dominica returns not one per cent. of the money laid out on it.

We have obferved, that 20,000 new flaves coft in three years £ 1,04000. But, in three years time, according to Long, vol. 2. p. 434. a third part is dead. We have then 13,700 flaves, worth £ 1,040,000. To this we muft add three years expenfe of phyfic, feeding, cloathing, &c. This we will make only £ 10 on the original number of 20,000, or £ 200,000. We have then 13,700

flaves

flaves which coft the planter £1,240,000 or £90 each flave. The reader will obferve, that in the firft eftimate, the expenfe of feeding the flaves, &c. at £5 per head, is thrown among the current expenfes. But here, where we eftimate the value of the flaves, it is an addition to their value, till they become ufeful. Thefe calculations are founded on the Planter's own conceptions, or on eftimates which he muft admit. They may be varied, but the conclufion will come out nearly the fame. Particularly no juft eftimate can be framed of the expenfe of new flaves, that makes not the furvivors exceed £90 in value. Long, vol. 2. p. 435. fuppofes that often one half dies. This would raife each of the furvivors to £124. In many cafes, in our new iflands, it has been two-thirds. In one within my own knowledge, had the remnant of flaves been fold each for £400, the owner would have been a lofer. In the moft favourable cafe that can be put, the furvivors of African flaves never pay for the coft and expenfe of the whole lot. We have obferved the unproductive labour of flaves, valued only at £50. When valued at £90 or more, the lofs will be more confiderable. Three flaves at £90 are worth £270. Their rent and infurance at this high value cannot be fo low as £12 each, or in all, £36. But the two hhds. of fugar produced by them are worth only £24, after paying current expenfes. There are £12 loft on the rent, and £18 loft on the lands, &c. occupied by them. If thefe calculations be difputed, it is hoped the Planter will correct them, by ftating them in his own way. I have gone by the beft information I could procure.

We may therefore conclude, that no new importation of new flaves can turn out profitably to

the

the planter; but as Long acknowledges, vol. 2. p. 437. muft form only a new addition to his debts and difficulties. Therefore, the abolition of the flave trade, far from giving the planter a claim to compenfation, will really fave him. Government will prevent him from continuing to involve himfelf unneceffarily in bankruptcy and ruin. The only means by which he can improve his condition is, as Long advifes, to ufe prudent regulations in the right hufbanding of his ftock, and promoting its increafe by natural means.

But indeed the annual fupply of new flaves, which in any cafe, with all its confequences, can hardly be fet below a million in value, is fuch a drain as no profit can admit of; nor can any poffible reduction in the produce fuppofed to follow the abolition of the flave trade, affect the planter's profit equally with this annual drain; fo that it muft be a profitable meafure, which at any hazard cuts it off. The fum paid for new flaves, if faved, would allow of encouragement to white people for domeftics and artifans, that where there is a want of flaves to keep up the full cultivation of the eftate, domeftic flaves may be turned into the field to make up the deficiency.

It appears that the Creole flaves, where the fexes are proportioned to each other, according to Long's eftimate of three flaves to two hogf-heads, without taking the Africans into account, may increafe the prefent produce, even in the liberal eftimate of 250,000 hhds. at which we have fet it (for the rum is included here in the making of fugar to make up that quantity of produce, and requires hardly any extra number of flaves) and may not only keep up, but increafe their numbers. Therefore, if the planter be not his own enemy, he needs not come to government

for

for relief, or go to the flave-market for recruits; his crops, his property, will not be affected. He will need no compenfation. The public treafury needs not be opened to reimburfe the 60 millions Weft-Indian property, with the annihilation of which we are threatened.

But it is faid, the revenue will annually lofe two millions; becaufe no fugar will be imported. Suppofe not an ounce of fugar imported, our ability to pay taxes would not on that account be leffened. Allow the revenue, freight, &c. on fugar to be two millions, and the fugar itfelf to be worth four millions. The Britifh confumers then pay fix millions for fugar. If no fugar were ufed, he could then pay government fix millions inftead of two. If any thing be ufed for fugar, a revenue may be raifed on that article. If we have foreign fugar, government may increafe the tax, becaufe it will come one-third cheaper than from our own colonies. The planter is not to fuppofe he contributes one farthing of thefe two millions, any more than the Emperor of China does of the commutation tea-tax; except for the confumption of fugar in his own family refiding in Britain. The confumer pays the tax. Sugar is only the medium by which it is raifed on the public. The like ruin to the revenue was predicted, when America threatened to withhold her tobacco; but we have experienced no fuch effect from the meafure.

Again, the abolition of the flave trade will ruin the Weft-Indian trade, which will ruin our marine, p. 22. I truft the Weft-Indian trade is in no danger. But fuppofe the one annihilates the other. We fhall, by abandoning the flave trade, fave more feamen than the other employs. The African flave trade deftroys annually 2000 men; in ten years 20,000. The fugar colonies

may

may employ 12,000 feamen. The lofs here is 3 in 200. Suppofe annually 200, in ten years 2000. The whole number of men employed in the Weft India trade in ten years, is 14,000. But in this time 20,000 are loft in the flave trade. If both were annihilated, in ten years we fhould fave 6000 men.

I truft I have removed effectually the fear of a demand to be made on the treafury for 60 millions Weft-India property to be annihilated by the abolition of the flave trade. I have on the contrary proved, that the planter will not be injured, but relieved ; or if injured, that he muft blame his own feverity and avarice. I have proved, and fhall farther prove, that commerce will not be hurt, that the revenue or fhipping need not be leffened. In fhort, that the meafure is agreeable to the demands of humanity and juftice, and alfo to the fuggeftions of prudence and political wifdom. One may blufh to think thefe fhould ever be placed in oppofition. The author of nature never intended to feparate them. They will never be found in oppofition, when every confequence is taken into account. Whatever is juft or honourable leads to profit and advantage, as well public as private. Muft a great nation be obliged to fend out robbers to deftroy and enflave an innocent people in a different quarter of the globe ; or fet thefe on to deftroy and enflave each other for the increafe of its revenue? Can any advantages fo procured turn out well at the laft? This traffick fteels the heart againft every human feeling; it corrupts the mind, and, if continued, will prove a canker to eat into our profperity and importance.

In combating the Weft-India planter's reafoning, I preferve the utmoft refpect for his candour.

B   I truft

I truft I fhall have pleafed him in fhewing that that juftice and humanity, which he generoufly acknowledges to be on the fide of the abolition contended for, are not at variance with political rights or worldly prudence. He himfelf favours the plan, if the planter's intereft could be fecured. The whole depends on the circumftance of new flaves being a profitable or lofing purchafe. Long agrees with me in their having been found a lofing bargain near twenty years ago. Since that they have advanced near one third in value, and every expenfe about them is increafed. What is the fair conclufion which he makes? that the purchafe much haften the ruin of every involved planter.

In ftating the following objections, I have collected from every quarter whatever I have found urged on the fubject, and have given the moft direct anfwers, each in its refpective place. To preferve brevity, I have been as careful as poffible to give no more on each head, than is neceffary to obviate the objection in its moft direct fenfe.

I fhall here remark, that till it can be fairly proved by the planter, in oppofition to the reafoning here ufed, and the authority of Long, that African flaves are, generally fpeaking, a profitable purchafe; no argument for the continuance of the flave trade, as far as it may affect our colonies, can have any weight on political confiderations. And though this fhould be indifputably proved, and no anfwer here given fhould be fuftained as valid, yet ought the flave trade to be abolifhed, as long as its advocates allow, " that it is unjuft to enflave negroes," that people, in refpect of us, innocent, are dragged from their homes and families, are murdered by a thoufand deaths,

by

by chains, confinement, fuffocating air, cruel treatment; that they are forcibly tranfported to diftant iflands, where not one in ten takes root, and there made to drawl out a wretched exiftence in inceffant labour without food, without clothes, without reft, under the capricious treatment of any fort of mafter, or any unfeeling boy that may be fet with a whip over them.

If we allow that power may confer right, may ftifle a brother's groans, and trample on every unalienable privilege of human nature, let us boldly declare it, and fend out fleets and armies, wherever refiftance is not expected, wherever flaves may be feized, and plunder or revenue may be acquired. It is now only that this object has caught the public attention. Hitherto we have fuffered ourfelves to be perfuaded, by inte-refted men, without inquiry, of the advantage and propriety of this inhuman traffic. But after this open difcuffion, we cannot poffibly go back. We will not, furely, permit certain murder to be carried on; and we cannot pretend to regulate a traffic, which is founded on murder, and cannot be feparated from it. Should we permit this traffic to be continued, we declare ourfelves to be the general enemies of mankind; we are to be confidered as a nation of robbers, and deferve to be fufpected and held in abhorrence, and guarded againft by every furrounding and diftant ftate.

J. R.

OBJEC-

OBJECTIONS

TO THE

Abolition of the Slave Trade,

WITH

ANSWERS.

Objection 1. *THE planter will ſhew his reſentment of the meaſure, by treating his ſlaves more cruelly than before.*

Anſwer 1. The ſudden diminution of his property, in conſequence of ſuch treatment, will diſcover to him the prudence of accommodating himſelf to his new ſituation, and the neceſſity of treating his ſlaves with humanity.

Object. 2. *The ſugar colonies will throw themſelves into the arms of France.*

Anſw. 2. Then will Britain be freed of the expenſe of their protection, and be able to procure plenty of ſugar at two thirds of the preſent price. Planters complain that they can hardly cultivate their plantations, while enjoying the monopoly of

the

the Britiſh market, How will they bear the reduction of one third of its value in the markets of
their new maſters, for that is the ordinary proportion of the price of French ſugars?

Object. 3. *Planters in debt will carry their ſlaves
to the Spaniſh colonies.*

Anſw. 3. This may be left to the vigilance of
their creditors.

Object. 4. *Sugar cannot be procured from foreigners.*

Anſw. 4. While ſugar is made, Britiſh money
will command it. Foreign ſugars, near one third
cheaper than Britiſh, have long found their way
into our colonies, The importation may be extended, but it will not be neceſſary. Indeed ſugar might be brought from the Eaſt-Indies, made
by free men, much cheaper than ſlaves can poſſi-
bly produce it in the Weſt-Indies. Good clayed
ſugar is ſold in Batavia by the cwt. for about 13s.
Arrack made from it is worth only 8d. per gallon.
Theſe prices would allow of the expenſe of freight
to Europe, and the ſugar to be ſold at 3d. per
pound in England. In Cochin China it is made
even at half this price.

Object. 5. *The planter will prove the abſurdity
of the meaſure, by increaſing the ſeverity of his manner
of treating his ſlaves.*

Anſw. 5. When he finds his property hurt by
ſuch a ſtep, he will deſiſt from his unfeeling conduct.

Object. 6.

Object. 6. *Involved planters will waste their slaves by excessive exertions.*

Answ. 6. Excessive exertions have constantly proved ruinous. Nor can the necessity of making such exertions be avoided by the introduction of new slaves; because they cannot possibly be made (see introduction) to repay their first cost, expense and loss in seasoning. Still the involved planter shuts his eyes, and goes on, though every example around him solicits him to abandon the vain attempt.

Object. 7. *The neutral islands were settled, and their lands bought in a confidence, that government would continue to permit the importation of slaves.*

Answ. 7. The sale of these lands has been closed near twenty years. If any of them be unsettled, they never can henceforth be profitably settled by African slaves; for they never repay their own cost, and therefore cannot contribute to clear lands and erect buildings. The truth is, that the lands now remaining uncultivated, have not generally been paid for, or have been abandoned as unprofitable.

Object. 8. *Parliament has given its sanction to the trade by regulating it.*

Answ. 8. If the countenance given by parliament to this horrid trade, has constantly been procured by the representations of interested people, must government be charged with the consequences arising from the imposition. Because we had laws that once fixed a commutation for murder, were we thereby precluded from ever improving

our

our police ? But this fhews how cautious we fhould be, by any regulation, to give a fanction to op-preffion and murder.

Object. 9. *A religious fociety is poffeffed of a plantation in Barbadoes, and employs flaves.*

Anfw. 9. It holds the Codrington eftate for particular purpofes, on condition of keeping up a certain number of flaves. Like other abfent pro-prietors, it has fuffered by the mifmanagement of fervants. It is now in a train to anfwer both the intentions of the donor, and the wifhes of huma-nity.

Object. 10. *The treatment of horfes fhould be regulated at home, before we look to Africa.*

Anfw. 10. When we have vindicated the rights of our fellows, it is to be hoped horfes will be confidered; for doubtlefs they are an object of police. But doth not this fhew, that a flave is efteemed a mere beaft of burden.

Object. 11. *To imprifon debtors, and imprefs men to ferve in war, are violations of moral law, equally with domeftic flavery.* Confideration, p. 28.

Anfw. 11. He who runs in debt knows the confequences; but all is a force upon the poor negroe. Many men enter into the fea or land fer-vice willingly; and thofe who are impreffed are treated as volunteers are. But we never heard of an African offering himfelf to be received into a flave fhip; nor when he was forced on board, of having been put on a footing with the fhip's crew. But the impreffed failor, he is among his country-men,

men, and ferves his country. What common tie fubfifts between an African, living 1200 miles from the fea coaft, and a Weft-Indian planter, to induce him to fubmit to be tied neck and heel, to die a thoufand fuffocating deaths on fhip board; to go and be beaten, half ftarved, and abufed, in the cultivation of a plant, from which he reaps no profit?

Object. 12. *The agitation of this queftion will raife a rebellion among the flaves.*

Anfw. 12. Helplefs wretches. Their fpirits are too much broken down to think of rebellion. But if it be fufpected, let the planters, inftead of moving heaven and earth to prevent their relief, come nobly forward, and propofe a plan for their protection. They will blefs and cheerfully ferve them.

Object. 13. *Slaves cannot be trufted with arms.*

Anfw. 13. They have formed a part of the militia in Barbadoes, and have been found faithful. This would univerfally be the cafe, were they advanced in fociety. They acquire the emulation of Britons, and would exert themfelves in their caufe, had they privileges or property to contend for.

Object. 14. *Negroes are an inferiour race of beings.*

Anfw. 14. Every man of candour acquainted with them will deny this. But fuppofe it, will thofe who plead for laws in favour of horfes, maintain that negroes are to be trepanned, murdered

by

by thousands, and enslaved for the indulgence of our avarice?

Object. 15. *Leo Africanus describes the negroes of his time, Anno 1500, as brutish, and then sold for slaves, before the commencement of the present traffick.*

Answ. 15. He says the shepherds and mountaineers, of all the different African nations, as well as negroes, were brutish; but that the people of the plains and cities were polished, having arts, sciences, and laws among them. He visited only the settlements along the Senegal branch of the Niger, and says the countries southward were possessed by rich industrious people, great lovers of justice and equity. He mentions the kings of Tombuto and Burno, two negroe states, as going to war to take slaves to be sold to merchants, trading to Ægypt and the Mediterranean cities. But do we argue for slavery, because at all times the strong have enthralled the weak? Because Joseph was sold by his brethren, was Pharoah vindicated for enslaving the whole Hebrew nation? Or are we to continue for ever to encourage negroes to kidnap each other to be sold to us, because 300 years ago the king of Tombuto kidnapped and sold his neighbours?

Object. 16. *Supplies from Africa are necessary to keep up the stock.*

Answ. 16. Because planters prefer the hopes (I deny they ever possess the substance) of present profit to future advantage; and commit their affairs to managers, who, being not concerned in what may happen thirty years hence, prefer the buying to the breeding of slaves. Hence we may
judge

judge how far to believe them, when they fay they favour population. But ftop the trade, and their opinion and practice will both be changed. That increafe of flaves from the births, which accompanies humane treatment on every plantation, in every ifland where now practifed, will then be general. But wherefore fhould we go to Africa for flaves? Why not to France, Spain, or Italy? It would be equally lawful, and the little oppofition we might meet with, would encourage a military fpirit among us, without the expenfe of fleets or armies.

Object. 17. *Small plantations in debt will be abandoned, or united to others.*

Anfw. 17. It is the beft thing that can happen both to debtor and creditor; for fuch never pay intereft money; nor indeed do they fupport themfelves, except where the planter is out of debt, and lives with his flaves, planting provifions for himfelf and them, and being contented to fend to market as much fugar as an attention to thefe objects permit, to purchafe what his plantation affords not.

Object. 18. *Large plantations will fend lefs fugar to market.*

Anfw. 18. In every plantation much land is put in canes that pays not for the culture. Perhaps one fourth part of St. Kitts is in this fituation, and a much greater proportion in fome other colonies. Turn this into provifions for the flaves, and grafs for the cattle; fewer flaves will do the work, and the reduced quantity of land referved for the canes, getting more manure, will ftand
the

the weather better, and produce more certain and better crops.

Object. 19. *The importation of sugar, and its revenue, will be affected.*

Answ. 19. The importation of sugar will never be profitably increased (see introduction) by the purchase of African slaves; and we have proved that the revenue depends not on the quantity of sugar made in our own colonies; for we may raise the same, or higher duties, on foreign sugars. (See introduction, and object. 4.)

Object. 20. *The consumption of British commodities in the islands will be lessened.*

Answ. 20. The consumption of the sugar colonies is hardly half the consumption of half a million of people in a distant quarter of the globe. But the abolition will greatly increase it. For the slaves must be better supplied than hitherto with necessaries; and as they advance in society they will increase in their demands.

Object. 21. *The cultivation of the cane will be diminished.*

Answ. 21. So it may, and yet the quantity of sugar, and the profit from it, be increased, if only what pays for the culture (Object. 18.) be used; lands producing less than an hogshead per acre, hardly pays for the culture. Our islands contain about four millions of acres. A crop is taken from the same land every second year; from some fresh lands every year; 120,000 acres of good land selected for each crop, might give from

180,000

180,000 to 200,000 hogfheads, which exceeds a medium crop at prefent. According to Long's eftimate, 200,000 hogfheads may be made by 300,000 flaves, without leffening their numbers. A much lefs number properly fed, worked and affifted with cattle, would be fufficient.

Object. 22. *The new iflands require new flaves, and plantations underhanded may be improved by them.*

Anfw. 22. Hardly has one plantation in the new iflands given the loweft ufual intereft on its coft and expenfes. But the price of African flaves is now advanced fo high (Object. 19) that henceforth no purchafe of them can poffibly turn out profitable. The value of a negroe's labour, arguing from Long's eftimate, vol. 2. p. 437, 438, of three flaves to two hhds. can be reckoned only at £8. But the ufual rent and infurance of a flave, is from £10 to £12, and there is nothing left for the returns of the lands, &c. occupied by them. If ever, from this time, new lands be brought into culture, fome other method, than this of working them by African flaves, muft be tried. Let the planter twift the calculation as he pleafes, he will never prove a new flave profitable.

Object. 23. *The planter can bear no interruption in the annual fupply of flaves.*

Anfw. 23. In the late war he bore the interruption for about fix years, without any fenfible injury. Since that time he has made but fmall ufe of the trade, but though in his own power, has turned it over to the French and Spaniards. There is an accommodating difpofition in man,
that

that adapts itſelf to neceſſity. This meaſure indeed will only keep the planter, even in the opinion of Long, from running in debt.

Objeƈt. 24. *The planter will be ruined.*

Anſw. 24. Not one will be injured (Objeƈt. 6.
22, 23.) whoſe ruin is not already ſealed. He who
is not in debt, will accommodate himſelf to his
ſituation. He will throw out, or fallow his poor
grounds. He will manure better what remains.
He will allot lands for proviſions and graſs. He
will uſe the aſſiſtance of cattle. He will work
ſlaves not as hitherto againſt time, but a certain
taſk of work. He will allow them food, reſt, and
clothing. He will hire white people, or free negroes and mulattoes (of whom there are great
numbers in the colonies, without employment)
for domeſtics, and turn his ſlaves into the field.
He will buy up around him for the culture of the
cane, thoſe ſlaves that are now employed in leſs
produƈtive labour, or that belong to poor free
people, who are kept poor and idle, depending on
their ſlaves induſtry. This plan is alſo the beſt
that the involved planter can purſue, unleſs he
can ſell his ſlaves and other property to a more
wealthy neighbour. Thus by being prevented
from purchaſing new ſlaves, many may be forced
to methods of humanity, and ſaved from otherwiſe
inevitable ruin.

Objeƈt. 25. *A ſugar plantation is a profitable
manufaƈtory.*

Anſw. 25. It is an expenſive loſing one. It
will in no caſe ſucceed, but on a large ſcale, where
it can have within itſelf proviſions, recruits of
ſlaves

flaves and cattle. Even few of the moft profitable could bear to be brought to calculation, if
their expenfes were carried on from the firft purchafe.

Obje&. 26. *White men cannot work in a Weft-
Indian climate.*

Anfw. 26. Nor white nor black can fupport
unremitting labour, without food or reft. But
white men kept from new rum, may, in the morn-
ing and evening, perform double the prefent tafk
of flaves, without fuffering from the climate.
Barbadoes, St. Kitts, and Nevis, were originally
fettled by white men. It was only on the intro-
du&ion of negroes, that they began to decreafe in
numbers. But the mortality could not poffibly
have been greater among them than has been
lately in the new iflands, and in clearing frefh
lands in Jamaica.

Obje&. 27. *Nor will they work with flaves.*

Anfw. 27. Poor white men do work along
with their flaves. The beft fortunes that have
been eftablifhed in the Weft-Indies, have been by
thofe, who firft worked to buy, and then fhared
labour with a flave. There is, I believe, a baro-
net now alive, whom his mother tied on her back,
while fhe fed the mill with canes. The author
got acquainted with a Frenchman in St. Vin-
cent's, who began with his two hands, and fettled
and ftocked in fucceffion, five coffee plantations.

Obje&. 28. *Free negroes or mulattoes will not
work with flaves in the field.*

Anfw. 28.

Anfw. 28. Then hire them as domeftics, and turn domeftic flaves into the field. The colonies at prefent contain twice as many flaves as are neceffary, if properly affifted, treated and worked, to fend the prefent produce to market; and any fupply of labourers, if really wanted, is preferable to the African flave trade. Nor can an objection to the turning of domeftics and others into the field, be made by him, who propofes to go to Africa to kidnap, or encourage others to kidnap, and force happy free people from their native country, to die a thoufand deaths in their paffage to the Weft-Indies, that perhaps one in ten may work in his field a half ftarved flave.

Object. 29. *Slaves are neceffary as domeftics, and handy craftfmen.*

Anfw. 29. A flave handy-craftfman, performs not one third of the ordinary tafk of a freeman. But white handy-craftfmen may be increafed as wanted. Families entertain from 20 to 60 flaves, who do not the work of 5 or 6 hired fervants. The whole number of tradefmen, domeftics and others, not employed about fugar in the colonies, may be eftimated at 150,000. Thefe being effective people, and worked in the field, well fed, properly tafked and affifted by cattle, might of themfelves fend more than the prefent quantity of fugar to market. This exchange from the houfe to the field, often takes place from caprice, as a punifhment; and handy-craft flaves are occafionally fent in there. In any cafe, the exchange cannot encroach fo much on the rights of humanity, as the flave trade to Africa.

Object. 30.

Object. 30.   *No supply can be found if the trade be abolished.*

Answ. 30.   This is answered (Object. 27, 28, 29.) Perhaps not more than one half of the effective flaves in our colonies is actually employed in the culture of the cane.   There is then in the colonies a fufficient fupply of field flaves, till the encouragement of population shall have taken effect.

Object. 31.   *Slaves are happier than English peasants.*

Answ. 31.   Have peafants their eyes beat out, their bones broken, their flesh furrowed by the whip, their wives expofed to a bailiff's luft; are they, without remedy, confined to any, the moft unreafonable oppreffive mafter ?   Are their wives and children taken from them, and fold to diftant parts ?   Do they cultivate barren fpots of ground on Sundays for food ?   Is their daily allowance fix ounces of flour ?   Have they no warm clothing; no linen to wrap their new-born babe in ?   But it is endlefs to mark the difference.   The affertion infults common fenfe.

Object. 32.   *Negroes are happier in the colonies than in Africa.*

Answ. 32.   Pofitively denied.   Do they ever offer themfelves to be received into our flave fhips, to efcape from their wretched country ?   Is there not a charm in the place of nativity, that makes to the natives, Greenland more defirable than the polifhed parts of Europe ?   Do they not feize every opportunity of rifing againft, or ef-

C   caping

caping from their oppreffors? Do they not in-creafe in their own country, and decreafe in our more defirable colonies? For one moment fup-pofe this true. For one that lives to fettle in the Weft-Indies, ten are killed, fuffocated, or loft to Africa. To make one man happy, muft ten be deftroyed? But how can wretched Africa bear an annual lofs of 200,000 people in the prime of life, at which the flave trade and its confequences may be fairly eftimated, while happy Weft-In-dians (by the report of the African merchant, a writer on the planter's fide) require an annual fup-ply of 40,000, or nearly one tenth of the whole? This objection is advanced for a particular purpofe, and is exaggerated. But we know certainly that little and very cafy labour fupplies them with food and clothing in Africa; unceafing labour ftarves them in the Weft-Indies. Indeed, how can they be faid to be happy in a country, who, in feveral iflands, have not a fcrap of land allotted for their main-tenance, that can be turned to any other cul-ture?

Object. 33. *The labour of flaves is cheaper than that of free men.*

Anfw. 33. Moft pofitively denied. The plant-er affirms, that it requires fix flaves to do the work of one peafant. The moft pinching allow-ance that can be given to a flave, and the loweft eftimate his rent and infurance can be laid at, muft amount to a much larger fum, than the bare handy labour of any peafant, without cattle and inftru-ments of hufbandry, could poffibly perform. But it has been proved (See introduction) that the labour of a flave pays not for his coft and expenfe in feafoning. A mafter muft fupply the death of

a flave

a flave at an enormous expenfe from the flave-market. For a little better food and clothing, in return for a double tafk of work, the peafant, without coft, breeds labourers in fucceffion for his employers. But when it is acknowledged that flaves do lefs work than peafants, (if they do it cheaper, then they earn lefs in the fame time, and have therefore lefs means to buy the comforts of life) how then can they be happier than Englifh peafants, for example, (Object. 31.) who earn fo much more by their labour, and therefore have more the means of indulgence?

Object. 34. *Emancipation of flaves will ruin the mafter.*

Anfw. 34. It is not even fuggefted, (See introduction) till their improvement fhall have made it the mafter's intereft freely to beftow it. The fimple abolition of the trade, operating as a kind neceffity on the intereft and difcretion of the planter, and taking away this delufive lure from fhort-fighted avarice, will do every thing at prefent for the flave, that humanity requires. If any abufes remain, they may be regulated as difcovered, without injury to the mafter's property, or his juft authority over it.

Object. 35. *If freed they will not work.*

Anfw. 35. This conclufion is drawn from the indolence of favages. But it is not propofed to free them, till they fhall have been civilized, and prepared for the government of law. To fuppofe that in fuch circumftances they will not exert themfelves to procure the conveniences and comforts of life, in the fame manner as other civilized

C 2   people,

people, is to deny them the attributes of human nature. But there are many particular inftances in the colonies to contradict the fact; and in North America many planters have emancipated their flaves, and afterwards hired them to work by the day or piece, and found their advantage in it. The colliers in Scotland have been lately freed, to the mutual benefit of mafter and fervant. But indeed the objection is a mere conjecture, for very few have ever been freed in the Weft-Indies, on which the obfervation could be properly made.

Object. 36. *Theft is lightly punifhed in the colonies.*

Anfw. 36. Not always. I have myfelf feen fuch inftances of punifhment on bare fufpicion, as would make humanity fhudder. But what muft be the heart of that man, who can punifh with feverity a wretch, breaking a cane, or ftealing to fatisfy that hunger, which his parfimony has occafioned. Indeed the breaking of canes in my time, was a kind of high treafon, to be punifhed with particular feverity.

Object. 37. *Planters are mifreprefented; therefore probably Guinea captains are fo likewife.*

Anfw. 37. If the planter's own confcience condemns him not, we bring not his character into the queftion. Without quoting names, cruel facts are alledged as connected with flavery. But the reputation of planters and Guinea captains, are not touched on. There are good men in both lines. It is the oppreffion and murder of friendlefs leſs Africans, for whom the publick attention is claimed.

Objeƈt. 38. *A profit is drawn from the ſlaves ſold to foreigners.*

Anſw. 38. Here the intereſt of the ſlave mer-chant and of the planter diſagree. French planters particularly, not having much intereſt-money to pay, and managing their own planta-tions, can allot more of their produce to the increaſe of their ſtock, and give higher prices than our planters are willing to ſpare from their own perſonal expenſes. The French planter does not any more than the Engliſh make an ordinary intereſt of his money by the purchaſe of new ſlaves; but he prefers this method of appropriat-ing his income to that of ſpending it on his own perſonal indulgencies.

Objeƈt. 39. *If profitable for the French to buy, why not for us ?*

Anſw. 39. The French iſlands being more fertile than ours, can bear a more expenſive culti-vation; and their ſlaves being better fed and clothed, though unproduƈtive, are not ſo much ſo as our ſlaves. Of 800,000 ſlaves imported into St. Domingo in 96 years preceding 1774, there remained 140,000 Creoles, or one Creole from ſix Africans. Our whole number of Creoles would not be perhaps in the proportion of one from 12 Africans imported into our colonies.

Objeƈt. 40. *The French having no longer a com-petition with us, will buy their ſlaves cheap if we abandon the trade.*

C 3

Anſw.

Anfw. 40. In all fettled trades the profit foon becomes to be nearly equally diftributed among all thofe who are concerned in it. When an article has once fettled at a certain price, it can hardly ever be reduced back to its original coft, even when that circumftance is removed, which firft occafioned the rife. The tax on glafs is faid to have been doubled on the confumer. Repeal the tax, the price would not be diminifhed in proportion. Slaves, befides the expenfes of the fhip, which are £ 8 more, now coft in goods, on the coaft of Africa, at a medium about £ 17. Paffing through a variety of hands from the inland countries, in each of which a profit muft be left, any reduction of price on the coaft muft make flaves a lofing bargain, therefore the reduction of the price will counterbalance the want of competition. A manufacturer, who lofes part of his cuftomers, produces goods only fufficient to fupply his leffened demand, and muft try to lay a higher price on them, to make up for the lofs of his former trade. But if we can fhew that the flave trade is at beft precarious, and often a lofing trade, fhould the demand for flaves only change hands from us to the French, then will the French only extend a lofing traffick. If the demand be leffened, then will the flave-brokers quantum of profit be leffened, which the prefent ftate of the trade will not bear. This leaves us to conclude, that the French cannot draw great advantages from our abandoning the trade to them.

Obferv. 41. *If we give up the trade, the French will extend their fhare of it.*

Anfw. 41. Suppofe that others fuccefsfully rob and murder on the highway, muft we join the lawlefs band. At prefent, the French buy many
flaves

flaves on the coaft from our brokers. Our goods
pay for them, our factories accommodate them.
Stop thefe channels, and the French cannot at
once eafily fupply the goods, or procure the flaves.
To us it is (by the acknowledgment of men well
acquainted with the trade, when they have not a
particular point to carry) a precarious, and on the
whole, a lofing trade. Did one company carry it
on, that company muft become bankrupt. But
their prefent fhare has fo few allurements for their
own merchants, that their government offers a
bounty to Englifh fhips to be employed in it under
French papers for the fettlement of new lands in St.
Domingo. Still the French planter complains of
the hardfhip impofed on him by the advanced price
of flaves. Therefore, if the French extend their
trade, they will extend their lofs, efpecially of feamen, which extraordinary as ours (fee int.) is, greatly exceeds our proportion. In the mean time, it is
a fubject of difcuffion for government, to determine how far an eagernefs for lucre may be
indulged in our traders, when directed to the
improvement of a rival colony, with a view to
the eftablifhment of a marine, though at the
expenfe of the individual planters who pufh it
on. In another point of view, if the fubject be
properly propofed, may we not fuppofe the French
as capable as we are of being influenced by fen-
timents of humanity and juftice?

Object. 42. *This abolition will raife difputes on
the coaft of Africa with the French.*

Anfw. 42. The limits of our factories are
eftablifhed. Where the French hitherto have
not been permitted to buy flaves, they cannot
expect to be indulged to the hindrance of our
C 4 traffic

traffic in wood, gums, ivory, gold, &c. From their want of factories, they cannot extend their slave-trade. If the minds of the natives be once pre-occupied in favour of the barter trade, they will not allow slave-brokers to pass, but at an expense, which the trade cannot bear. Perhaps the Dutch, Danes, and Portuguese, may be induced to follow our example. Then the slave trade could not be carried on to any great extent.

Object. 43. *Slaves will be smuggled in from other islands to ours.*

Answ. 43. Not at present, because our planters living in England cannot afford to give as high prices as foreigners give. Our planters now do not, or cannot, buy what they think the necessary supplies at the present advanced price; and if they did buy them, according to Long, they would find them an unprofitable purchase. Smuggled negroes cannot cost less than 20 per cent. above the present rate; how will our planters be able to afford this? But when smuggling is discovered, it may easily be prevented; it is not now necessary to suppose it.

Object. 44. *The trade is an extensive market for our manufactures.*

Answ. 44. We should blush to think, that in order to make it profitable, we are obliged to cheat the poor Africans with damaged goods, and false measure; (see Newton's Thoughts on Slave-trade). Every man who argues for such a trade, argues for the basest treachery and fraud that ever came to the gallows. If this trade were stopped, our present fair trade in the staple commodities of Africa,

Africa, might be indefinitely extended. The whole export is eftimated within £ 800,000 collected from a number of adventurers, often as the laft pufh, in hopes of a lucky hit, like a ticket in the lottery, to fave them from bankruptcy. Of this a confiderable part is bartered for ftaple articles, as wood, ivory, &c. and full one-third is faid to be Eaft-India goods. This eftimate is checked by the number of flaves purchafed by our traders on the coaft. That number annually is about 40,000, which, at £ 17 per head, is only £ 680,000. The expenfes of the voyage are £ 8 more, which are charged on thofe fold to the planter

Object. 45. *Guinea captains, furgeons, and officers, alone gain annually £ 50,000 in this trade, and one particular dealer in Guinea fhips made an immenfe fortune.*

Anfw. 45. Thefe are almoft all the people who make money in the trade. The captain and officers by their privilege flaves, who never die, and their commiffion on the cargo, muft always make money. The dealer in fhips alluded to, had a great number in the trade, and ftood his own infurer in a lucky period.

Object. 46. *Slaves once brought down from the inland parts of Africa muft be exported to prevent them from being murdered.*

Anfw. 46. Could the trade be ftopped in a moment, the abolition fhould at once take place. But as numbers for many months muft continue to be brought down to the coaft, it will require fome management to confine their fale to our own iflands, fhould our planters be fo much perfuaded of their utility, as to put themfelves to
fome

fome inconveniencies in order to purchafe them, that they may not be paffed to foreigners.

Object. 47. *Our planters have not credit to purchafe flaves.*

Anfw. 47. This muft not be urged by any planter refiding in England; for if he thinks the purchafe profitable, why allots he not his European expenfes to this purpofe?

Object. 48. *The trade is a nurfery for feamen.*

Anfw. 48. It is the very grave of feamen, deftroying more than all our foreign trade befides, often lofing by deaths, incurable difeafes, &c. two-thirds of thofe employed in it; and in the proportion of about eight to one of thofe loft in the barter or wood trade on the fame coaft.

Object. 49. *The Weft-Indian trade is moft profitable to this country.*

Anfw. 49. Then why is every fugar factor trying all he can to fhake off his connections with the fugar planters, or to confine them intirely to the fale of his fugars, and the fhipping of his ftores? Can any planter now borrow money on his Weft-Indian property, either to improve it, or pay off preffing demands? Has there not been more bankruptcies among capital houfes connected with the fugar colonies, than in any other branch of trade? Nay, it will be found, that the flave-trader himfelf complains of the tardinefs of the planter's payments.

Object. 50.

Object. 50. *Slaves muſt carry out dung in baſ-kets, and bring canes home in bundles.*

Anſw. 50. Allot lands for graſs, and one horſe and cart will do the work of forty ſlaves.

Object. 51. *In crop time, the whole gang, what-ever be its number, muſt be employed in making of the ſugar.*

Anſw. 51. Gangs of 220 ſlaves; others, not amounting to 100, are kept to the ſame work, with little difference in the quantity of ſugar made, that may not be explained from other circum-ſtances, as the ſituation of the mill for receiving the wind, &c. Here ſurely muſt be a waſte of labour in the more numerous gang; becauſe the other plantation work might alſo be carried on ſo as to make fewer ſlaves neceſſary at other times. The fact is, 140 or 160 ſlaves often cultivate as much land, and ſend as much ſugar to market as 220 ſlaves. Theſe laſt muſt therefore be ill managed.

Object. 52. *Slaves muſt be kept at work, or under command, from dawn till late at night.*

Anſw. 52. What purpoſe this drawling method anſwers, but the indulgence of caprice of avarice ill underſtood, cannot be diſcovered. Give them a taſk. They may reſt in the heat of the day, and do twice their preſent work. But they muſt be better fed, and not be ſent in the hour of reſt two miles from home to pick graſs for cattle.

Object. 53. *Slaves cannot be aſſiſted by cattle.*

Anſw. 53. The plough might be uſed in a
great

great proportion of cane land. But cattle may at leaſt aſſiſt always in carrying out dung and bringing home canes, as is now done on particular plantations. But ſuch is the avarice for ſugar, that no graſs lands are allotted for the ſupport of cattle. Hence often at the beginning of a crop, the whole ſtock of cattle muſt be renewed at any price.

Object. 54. *The ſtate of ſlaves will not be improved by the planting of proviſions.*

Anſw. 54. The culture of proviſions is eaſier than that of canes. Plant them where canes pay not for the culture. Expence is ſaved; the ſlaves are more plentifully fed, and the remaining cane land is better dreſſed, and becomes more productive.

Object. 55. *Proviſions muſt be brought from Europe and America to feed the ſlaves.*

Anſw. 55. This unnatural ſtate anſwers neither the purpoſe of profit or humanity. Slaves will never be well fed by grain brought from diſtant parts. In bad years, when the planter is leaſt able to purchaſe it, it will be moſt wanted. In the beſt years, luxury will grudge the coſt. In fact, ſlaves will never be well fed with ſuch purchaſed grain.

Object. 56. *Slaves have ſufficient proviſion ground.*

Anſw. 56. And, except in Jamaica, only Sunday to work it. But it is not generally true, either that they have ſufficient ground, or that it is generally

generally ufeful. A few prime flaves appropriate the beft parts, and weakly flaves are thruft out, or have their provifions ftolen. Hardly ever can they fpare them to ripen. Provifion ground will be ufeful only, when made, equally with cane land, the work of the whole gang under the overfeer. Yet this moft neceffary part of plantation economy is almoft wholly neglected, the manager thinking much once or twice in a feafon to examine into the ftate of it.

Object. 57. *Moft excellent orders are fent out by abfent planters.*

Anfw. 57. Whatever be their tenour, they are always interpreted by the cuftom of the colonies, which is for feverity and pinching. They are always fuppofed to mean, Send home as much fugar, and draw as few bills on them as poffible. A gentleman for fourteen years had defired the happinefs of his flaves, not revenue, to be confidered. But afking his managers why his flaves did not increafe under fuch orders, he received for anfwer, " they had been too hard worked, " and too ill fed ?"

Object. 58. *It is the planter's intereft to treat his flaves well.*

Anfw. 58. Then his practice contradicts his opinion, Can it be his intereft to allow his flave neither food or reft ? Are fix ounces of flour, or five hours reft, fufficient refrefhment for twenty-four hours ? Can it be his intereft to wear them out by inconfiderate fatigue, and in a few years be obliged repeatedly to renew his gang from the flave-market, rather than by difcreet management

to

to enable them to carry on his work, and raife up without expenfe, fucceffive generations of labourers for his profit.

Obje&t. 59. *The treatment of flaves fhould be regulated.*

Anfw. 59. Except in a very few points it is almoft impoffible for law to come between a mafter and his flave. A cruel or capricious man can teafe and wafte his flave in a thoufand ways that law cannot check, nor authority reach. The Danes, indeed, have an effe&tual method in their iflands, which has been enforced in feveral particular inftances. The governor divefts a cruel mafter of the management of his property, and fets humane people over it:—a cuftom truly worthy of imitation.

Obje&t. 60. *Plantations cannot be fupplied from the births.*

Anfw. 60. Nor will they while the flave-market is confidered as a better mode of recruiting them than that of population. But at prefent many increafe from the births in all the rice, tobacco, and fugar colonies, from the cafualty of a humane mafter, and eafy manager, a careful manager's wife, an attentive furgeon. This proves the ftrong biafs in nature to increafe where not checked by oppreffion ; and it would univerfally be the cafe if humane and proper treatment were univerfal.

Obje&t. 61. *Population is checked by an over proportion of males.*

Anfw. 61.

Anſw. 61. This over proportion takes place only among African ſlaves, who are not prolific in the colonies, not from natural cauſes, but from chagrin, the want of neceſſaries, and encouragement. But their proportion cannot at preſent be very conſiderable, (ſee introduƈt.) The natural proportion of the ſexes takes place among the Creoles, who are in ſufficient numbers, if properly indulged and aſſiſted, to overſtock all our iſlands in a few years, without diminiſhing the preſent produce of ſugar.

Objeƈt. 62. *Slaves are not kidnapped by our traders, but culprits or priſoners of war.*

Anſw. 62. We do not ſay that any great proportion of them are now kidnapped by our traders; becauſe as far as they can reach with their boats the country is either deſolated by former depredations, or is under ſuch police as makes it rather dangerous; though it ſometimes happens that we hear of a captain making what he calls a ſtroke, ſweeping away as many freemen as he can overpower with his crew. But we ſay that the natives kidnap each other, and that criminals make but a very ſmall proportion of the whole. That they are kidnapped is almoſt the univerſal anſwer from thoſe brought into our colonies; nor can the numbers brought down to the coaſt be accounted for in any other manner. But ſuppoſe them culprits or priſoners of war, are we then the executioners for African tyrants, or African judges? Are we to puniſh unfortunate wretches by the thouſand deaths endured in our ſlave ſhips? Offer a Guinea captain, condemned for murdering his crew or his ſlaves, his life, on condition of being fettered and treated as a ſlave

in

in the paſſage to the Weſt-Indies, he would run for refuge to the gallows. Moore mentions a free negroe offered to him for ſale for ſtealing a tobacco pipe. If priſoners of war may be enſlaved, why ſend we not our ſlave-traders to attend the Turkiſh and Ruſſian armies, and provide ourſelves there? It will be as juſt and proper, as to ſtir up wars in Africa for the purpoſe of making ſlaves.

Objeċt. 63. *Britain produces annually* 2000 *culprits. The negroe countries are four times as large. They therefore may ſupply annually* 80,000 *culprits.*

Anſw. 63. This ſuppoſes Africa equally civilized with Britain; for crimes are the offspring of civilization. Crimes exiſt not among ſavages. There muſt be laws and police to which they are to be referred. This, therefore, if true, cuts off another aſſertion, that the Africans are brutiſh. But how does our method of collecting ſlaves on the coaſt agree with this notion? Our traders ſhould demand a certificate of the ſlave's ſentence, leſt he take away an innocent perſon. The fact is, among imported ſlaves there exiſts no appearance of culprits: ſome are young girls not grown up; many boys under 14 years: they generally affirm themſelves to have been kidnapped. If criminals, ſome of their old practices would now and then break out; but they are quiet inoffenſive people, guilty only of brooding over their unhappy ſtate, or of ſtealing from a niggardly maſter to keep themſelves from dying of hunger.

Objeċt. 64. *They are the children of women kept for breeding ſlaves.*

Anſw. 64. Then they would be ſold when children;

children; but the flave cargoes confift of all ages of both fexes, which have been kidnapped or en-flaved in wars made on purpofe to accommodate the dealers in this horrid traffick.

Object. 65. *The king of Dahomy murders his peo-ple for his amufement, therefore we may traffick in flaves.*

Anfw. 65. This monfter, from fuperftition, fa-crifices his own people, and from avarice, enflaves and fells others. But the one paffion intermeddles not with the exertion of the other. Their opera-tions are diftinct. His avarice is encouraged by our traders, and renders numbers of his people wretch-ed, in addition to thofe lefs unhappy people, who are the victims of his cruelty. By checking this in-human trade, we fhould annihilate one half of the evil; by profecuting it, we are guilty of all the ills produced by it, and encourage his favage dif-pofition.

Object. 66. *The flaves are bought in open market, and the brokers will not difclofe any particulars refpect-ing their captivity.*

Anfw. 66. Do not our traders wink with their eyes, and avoid any clofe inquiry? But if they be ignorant how they are originally procured in the land parts, how come they fo well acquainted with the circumftances of their being the children of flave breeders, prifoners of war, and culprits? In-deed to call them culprits, contradicts another plea that they are brutifh; for among favages there can be no culprits. Society muft be well advan-ced before a man can be confidered as criminal, and an object of juftice.

D   *Object.* 67.

Object. 67. *Slaves are well cared for on board the flave ships, and lofe not above four in an hundred, in the paffage from Africa to the Weft-Indies.*

Anfw. 67. Where fix men are ftowed in the place of one, which is the difference between a flave-fhip and a tranfport for carrying troops, it is impoffible that the wretches can be well cared for. But for this, fee Mr. Newton and Mr. Fal-conbridge's accounts of their horrid ftate. It may have poffibly happened, that not more than four in an hundred, might in a particular cafe have been loft in the paffage. But what is this to the many inftances where an half, or even two-thirds, have been loft before the fhip had reached the Weft-Indies? If fo few be loft, how comes it that a flave-trader cannot get infurance in London on his flaves at any rate; or that thofe, who in one or two inftances under-wrote flaves at 25 per cent. premium, refufed to continue the advantageous bargain?

Object. 68. *They are encouraged to rear children, and will not.*

Anfw. 68. Can they rear them for him, who demands bricks without ftraw, that they may be oppreffed at his caprice? How few are put in the ftate, have food, clothes, or neceffaries, to encourage them, or are indulged when pregnant, or when nurfes? Can a young fingle lad, or a batchelor manager, as is now the growing cuftom to employ on plantations, have that fellow-feeling and fympathy with a child-bearing woman, that may be expected in a tender-hearted matron? I can recollect but one cafe, where flaves have increafed under a batchelor. There fome pecu-
liarly

liarly favourable circumſtances take place. Thoſe acquainted with the uſual treatment of ſlaves, may wonder how ſo many children are reared, rather than ſo few. Indeed, the ordinary cauſes of the increaſe of ſlaves on particular plantations, ſhew how eaſily population may be promoted.

Objeƈt. 69. *Negroe women are profligate, and deſtroy their fruit.*

Anſw. 69. This takes place among none but perhaps a few, that are ſuffered to work, or hire themſelves out among ſeamen.

Objeƈt. 70. *The number of Creoles, where the ſexes only are in due proportion, is not equal to the ſupport of the preſent ſtock.*

Anſw. 70. Denied, ſee Introduƈtion. Our Creoles exceed two-thirds of our preſent number of ſlaves; but not more than two-thirds of the whole are employed in the culture of ſugar, and that in a proportion, which Long ſays, they may continue to increaſe from the births. Every other department may eaſily be ſupplied by white men or free negroes, and mulattoes. It muſt not be loſt ſight of, that few African women breed, and that no new ſlaves repay their coſt, expenſe, and loſs in ſeaſoning. We cannot, therefore, ſuppoſe any future progeny of theſe capable of repaying the expenſe of ſuch a purchaſe; and can expeƈt a profitable recruit only from Creoles. But there are inſtances in every colony of humane treatment aƈtually producing an increaſe. This will univerſally be the caſe, when the praƈtice is univerſal.

Objeƈt. 71.

Object. 71. *Unhealthy situations require supplies.*

Answ. 71. Can this be urged by any man pretending to humanity or discretion. Abandon the cultivation of the cane, rather than sport with a brother's life. The unhealthiness of mines, &c. cannot be pleaded here, because worked by volunteers. But no plantation that requires supplies can repay the expense. We may still ask, Has every proper measure been adapted for the particular situation? Are the huts fixed in a dry airy spot? Are the slaves plentifully fed, discreetly worked, well defended with clothes against damps, or wet weather. Few situations are to be found that may not be corrected, so as that the human constitution shall adapt itself to it. But their manner of living must be that of proper inhabitants, not artificial, as in a garrison, or used as beasts of burden, and pretended to be fed with grain brought from other quarters of the globe.

Object. 72. *Slavery is not unlawful; the bible allows of it.*

Answ. 72. The use of money is not unlawful. But it is unlawful to rob on the highway to procure it. We meddle not with slavery, but with the ordinary means of procuring slaves. We say men ought not to go to the coast of Africa to kidnap the natives, or to encourage them to kidnap each other; or to bribe them with baubles to go to war, to fight with and enslave each other; to turn every trespass into a cause for enslaving; to subject the unfortunate wretches to the miseries of a West-Indian voyage; to sell them

them to be half-ftarved, hard worked, and ill treated.

Chriftianity obliges us to inftruct and inform the mind. Social liberty is the genuine confequence of improvement. Therefore we may fay, that the Chriftian privilege favours liberty; and, while it avoids making any fudden change in eftablifhed cuftoms, it naturally tends towards it.

Object. 73. *The Jews were permitted to hold flaves.*

Anfw. 73. They might keep the children of the heathen, and their pofterity, flaves. But they were enjoined to treat them well; inftruct them in their religion, and make them partakers of their religion and laws. The flaves were fupplied with food and clothing from their fix days labour, without being forced to work for this on Sabbath. If the mafter ftruck out but a tooth, the flave was to be free. If he took a maid-fervant to his bed, or gave her to his fon, fhe had the privilege of a wife, and could not be fold. We muft imitate the example of the Jews, if we claim their permiffion of holding flaves. But by the coming of our Saviour, all men are become brethren. A Jew could hold a Jew in fervice only for fix years, and only fuch as were too poor to maintain themfelves. We make the Africans poor by enflaving them. But we fhould keep them flaves only for fix years, and then difmifs them well fupplied with neceffaries. Farther, the Jews themfelves were numerous in a fmall country. Their flaves muft, therefore, have been few. Among thofe who returned from their captivity, there was but one flave to fix Jews; perhaps one fervant to each family.

Object. 74.

Object. 74. *Slavery renders oppreffion neceffary.*
See Niger *in* Public Advertifer *of March* 12.

Anfw. 74. But what except avarice renders
flavery neceffary ; and can oppreffion, if it be the
neceffary confequence of a vice, be in any degree
or fhape vindicated ? Murder is often the neceffary confequence of paffion. Is murder therefore
to be excufed ? What an opening is here for
crimes and villany of every fort.

Object. 75. *Free negroes and mulattoes do not*
increafe from the births.

Anfw. 75. It is not true, many inftances to
the contrary might be produced. But it is alfo
true, that no race or rank of men will continue
to increafe, except where the means of living are
in abundance. Thofe here defcribed, are exceed-
ingly fettered between white men on the one
fide, and flaves on the other, for the means of
fubfiftence. Therefore they cannot expand themfelves. It is fo with the native white people in
St. Kitt's ; their marriages are prolific, but from
the want of fubfiftence, the old families have in-
fenfibly vanifhed, and every year takes from the
population of the colony.

Object. 76. *A compenfation muft be made to*
Planters for 60 *millions of property, which the abo-*
lition of the flave-trade will annihilate.

Anfw. 76. It will be time enough to think of
compenfation when the lofs has been fuftained.
Even then I fhould proteft againft the claims of
fuch Weft-India appraifements as I have been
acquainted

acquainted with. Yet no planter, not already ruined, will fuffer by the abolition.

Compenfation would defeat every purpofe aimed. at, for procuring good treatment to the flaves. Many Planters find their affairs irrecoverable. If they hurry not on their fate, from the hopes of compenfation, at leaft they will be carelefs of the iffue. Their former inconfiderate conduct will continue, perhaps will be fharpened, to enhance their demand.

If there be a Planter, who has fed his flaves well, and worked them confiderately, has indulged them with proper reft, has clothed them properly, has furnifhed neceffaries for the encouragement of population, has lived with them, has treated them as fellow-creatures, has made the fupport of his plantation his prime object, and been contented with that revenue which this attention would admit of; in the name of juftice let him be liberally compenfated. But fuch a character fo circumftanced, fo unfuccefsful, is not to be found. The need of compenfation is a fure proof he deferves it not. Again, let it be obferved, that he claims this compenfation becaufe he is prevented from burying African flaves; which, even in Long's opinion, would only more involve him.

But if a man has feparated himfelf from his property, has drawn a revenue to fupport at a diftance an expenfive eftablifhment, from a property not equal to fuch demands, or which perhaps itfelf wanted fupplies; if, to force out this revenue, his half-ftarved flaves have been inceffantly worked; if neceffaries for the encouragement of population have been withheld, and the affiftance of cattle has been refufed; let not this man come to government to make up a lofs arif-

ing

ing from the cravings of luxury, or the inconfiderate ufe of power. In this clafs will be found
every Planter who has ruined himfelf by fpecu-
lating in fugar plantations. Mere adventurers
cannot claim compenfation, for they are where
they fet out. Their creditors have no claim; for
they took the chance of their fuccefs.

Objeƈt. 77. *The trade fhould be regulated, not
abolifhed.*

Anfw. 77. Regulate murder as you pleafe, it
ftill remains murder. Suppofe a regulation. It
muft check the mode of loading the flave-fhips.
But at prefent, with every contrivance in the
fhipmafter's power, it is on the whole a lofing-
trade; it depending on circumftances, whether a
particular fhip makes a faving voyage. Regulations which fhall make it more expenfive, will
make that lofs certain, which is now contingent.
Therefore, while holding out indulgence, they
will occafion a greater lofs, than the abrupt abolition of it.

But the regulations will be accepted with a
defign to evade them. In this cafe, the Legiflature becomes anfwerable for the oppreffion and
murder conneƈted with this trade.

CONCLUSION.

IF the fubjeƈt be difcuffed, the trade will be
found fo iniquitous, that it cannot be left on its
prefent footing, or be poffibly regulated. Let the
abolition then take place on the broad bafis of
humanity, juftice, and found policy. All particular circumftances will eafily accommodate themfelves to the new fituation of things.

POST-

POSTSCRIPT.

I SHOULD be ungrateful to pafs over the candour of the author of the Confiderations on Emancipation, &c. to myfelf. He has laid me under very great obligations, by ftepping forward to vindicate my reputation from the many horrid charges brought againft me by my former adverfaries ; efpecially, for clearing me of the crime of cruelty to my flaves, which has been circulated in every company where flavery has been agitated, and mentioned with as much abhorrence, as if no man befides me had been unfeeling in his treatment. He will allow me to obferve, that that irritation, which he makes the alloy of my temper, cannot be intolerable, if it permits me to be affectionate in my family, eafy to my flaves, and charitable to the poor; for to thefe the natural temper is leaft under difguife. He indeed takes out the fting, by charging my difputes to the pique and prejudice of my enemies. I may add, among thofe praifed in my Effay, are fome, who were then my inveterate foes. He will alfo indulge me in correcting his miftake concerning the M. Reviewers. Far from cenfuring injurious epithets in my writings, they blamed their want of warmth. From their late conduct I have only learned, that to utter falfe criminal libels againft Mr. R. in low vulgar language, is decent moderate conduct in his adverfaries; but it is abufe for him to ufe the moft cautious terms in his own vindication.

But p. 36. I am charged with mifreprefentation. If he will perufe my Effay, he will fee I prevent the conclufion of indifcriminate ill-treatment of

flaves,

flaves, by obferving, that arbitrary power in the mafter has not all thofe ill confequences with which fenfibility is apt to charge it. And if this, and many paffages of like import, be not fufficient to excufe me, I cheerfully embrace this opportunity of declaring, that the nature of flavery, not the difpofition of the mafter, is chargeable with the enormities connected with this debafing ftate. But he allows that there is occafion for cenfure, and that my book contains many truths, which he wifhes, for the honour of human nature, he could deny. Indeed, if it were not an invidious tafk, every circumftance in it might be referred to individuals, probably well known to this gentleman. I hope this is the laft time I fhall have occafion to mention myfelf, on a fubject, that ought not to be blended with the reputation of its advocates. But as I am tired of being obliged to carry about with me proofs of the innocency of my character, to vindicate it from the calumny caft upon it in every company, where my private intereft can be hurt, or the caufe in which I am engaged, injured ; and as this work may come into hands, which thefe Confiderations may not reach, I truft I fhall ftand excufed with the public for inferting from them here my own eulogium, mixed as it is with irritation of temper, and mifreprefentation of facts.

EXTRACT

EXTRACT from CONSIDERATIONS on
the Emancipation of Negroes, and on the Abolition of the Slave Trade, by a West-India
Planter, page 34, &c.

" HAVING introduced the name of this
" writer, (Mr. Ramsay) without whose labours
" the subject of slavery would not probably have
" been so much agitated at this day, I cannot dif-
" miss him without farther mention, as well to
" rescue his character from unmerited reproach, as
" to caution his readers against the exaggerations
" of his pen. As a husband and father he was
" affectionate and provident. As a pastor, de-
" cent, pious, temperate, and exemplary. As a
" master of slaves, so far was he from indulging
" in the exercise of cruelty, that he was remark-
" ably abstemious in the use of discipline, even on
" necessary occasions. He was charitable to the
" poor, and punctual in his pecuniary transactions.
" His good qualities were many; but at the same
" time, his temper was prone to irritation; and if
" not absolutely vindictive, he was at least ex-
" tremely liberal in the use of injurious epithets,
" as appears from his writings, which have drawn
" on him the correction of the learned Journalist,
" under whose review they have passed, though
" otherwise sufficiently disposed to favour his
" cause.
" Unfortunately his book was written during
" a state of warfare with his parishioners; a con-
" test unprovoked, it must be allowed by any act
" on his part, inconsistent with the character of a
" good man, but suggested by pique, and profe-
" cuted by party, on the other side. However, he
" has combined his own injuries with the inju-
" ries

" ries of the flaves, and given fcope to his refent-
" ment, while he appears an advocate in the caufe
" of humanity. That his book contains a great
" many truths, I wifh, for the honour of human
" nature, I could deny. Where authority exifts,
" it is too apt to be abufed. Slavery therefore
" neceffarily fuppofes fuch a ftate of oppreffion
" and confequent abafement, as is unpractifed
" among the free orders of fociety, and for a good
" reafon, becaufe it is untolerated. But to fup-
" pofe thofe oppreffions either fo frequent, or fe-
" vere as they are charged to be, would certainly
" be to give too great a degree of credit to his
" mifreprefentations.'

N. B. Page 40, he allows with me that French
flaves are better clothed and better fed than Englifh flaves ; a truth, which has been difputed with
me.

F I N I S.